CONTENTS

MW00763235

JESUS' DEATH & RESURRECTION

"**H**ey, what's up? You look pretty depressed for a Friday before vacation."

"I'm not looking forward to Easter."

"What? Easter means spring break—no school!"

"Oh, I like the break from school; I just feel down this time of year."

"Why? Easter reminds us that Jesus rose from the dead. That's something to celebrate, not get depressed about."

"I know. But that's not the depressing part. After Easter's over, I feel a big letdown. You know, an empty feeling."

"I'm not sure I follow you."

"Well, during Easter week we go from grieving about Jesus' death to celebrating his Resurrection in a matter of days— then we forget about it the rest of the year. Jesus' death and Resurrection seem too important to ignore 51 weeks out of the year."

"Maybe Easter should come more than once a year."

"Yeah, maybe so."

● ● ●

Make that "maybe so" a "definitely!"

The kids in the opening scenario are right on target. Jesus' death and Resurrection *are* too important to relegate to just one week out of the year. Easter should be a year-round celebration of God's new covenant with his people through Jesus' sacrifice.

The key to making Easter a year-round experience lies in kids' understanding of Jesus' death and Resurrection—and what it means for them.

Many teenagers don't know much more than the historical events of Jesus' death and Resurrection. By taking a tour of the events leading up to and following Jesus' death on the cross, kids can learn the significance of each event. As they sit down with Jesus at the Last Supper, they'll begin to understand the importance of remembering God's promises. As they pray with Jesus in Gethsemane, kids will see the value of a close relationship with God through prayer. As kids watch on the hillside while soldiers crucify Jesus, they'll discover the true meaning of sacrifice and forgiveness. And as they celebrate Jesus' Resurrection, kids will learn to live each day with Resurrection joy.

Teenagers can take that tour in your classroom. If you're holding this book, you're holding the tour map.

Jesus' Death & Resurrection will help kids turn a historical understanding of the events celebrated each Easter into a personal understanding they can relate to each day of the year.

By the end of this course your students will:
- learn how to be alone with God;
- explore Matthew's account of Jesus' death and Resurrection;
- commit to forgive others as Jesus forgives them;
- express their faith in Jesus boldly;
- understand the significance of Jesus' Resurrection for their lives; and
- celebrate Jesus' Resurrection.

COURSE OBJECTIVES

HOW TO USE THIS COURSE

ACTIVE LEARNING

Think back on an important lesson you've learned in life. Did you learn it from reading about it? from hearing about it? from something you experienced? Chances are, the most important lessons you've learned came from something you experienced. That's what active learning is—learning by doing. And active learning is a key element in Group's Active Bible Curriculum.

Active learning leads students in doing things that help them understand important principles, messages and ideas. It's a discovery process that helps kids internalize what they learn.

Each lesson section in Group's Active Bible Curriculum plays an important part in active learning:

The **Opener** involves kids in the topic in fun and unusual ways.

The **Action and Reflection** includes an experience designed to evoke specific feelings in the students. This section also processes those feelings through "How did you feel?" questions and applies the message to situations kids face.

The **Bible Application** actively connects the topic with the Bible. It helps kids see how the Bible is relevant to the situations they face.

The **Commitment** helps students internalize the Bible's message and commit to make changes in their lives.

The **Closing** funnels the lesson's message into a time of creative reflection and prayer.

When you put all the sections together, you get a lesson that's fun to teach—and kids get messages they'll remember.

BEFORE THE 4-WEEK SESSION

● Read the Introduction, the Course Objectives and This Course at a Glance.

● Decide how you'll publicize the course using the art on the Publicity Page (p. 9). Prepare fliers, newsletter articles and posters as needed.

● Look at the Bonus Ideas (p. 46) and decide which ones you'll use.

● Read the opening statements, Objectives and Bible Basis for the lesson. The Bible Basis shows how specific passages relate to senior highers today.

● Choose which Opener and Closing options to use. Each is appropriate for a different kind of group. The first option is often more active.

● Gather necessary supplies from This Lesson at a Glance.

● Read each section of the lesson. Adjust where necessary for your class size and meeting room.

BEFORE EACH LESSON

● The approximate minutes listed give you an idea of how long each activity will take. Each lesson is designed to take 35 to 60 minutes. Shorten or lengthen activities as needed to fit your group.

● If you see you're going to have extra time, do an activity or two from the "If You Still Have Time . . ." box or from the Bonus Ideas (p. 46).

● Dive into the activities with the kids. Don't be a spectator. The lesson will be more successful and rewarding to both you and your students.

HELPFUL HINTS

● The answers given after discussion questions are responses your students *might* give. They aren't the only answers or the "right" answers. If needed, use them to spark discussion. Kids won't always say what you wish they'd say. That's why some of the responses given are negative or controversial. If someone responds negatively, don't be shocked. Accept the person, and use the opportunity to explore other angles of the issue.

THIS COURSE AT A GLANCE

Before you dive into the lessons, familiarize yourself with each lesson aim. Then read the scripture passages.
- Study them as a background to the lessons.
- Use them as a basis for your personal devotions.
- Think about how they relate to kids' circumstances today.

LESSON 1: A MEAL TO REMEMBER

Lesson Aim: To help senior highers discover and remember God's promises.

Bible Basis: Exodus 12:1-30 and Matthew 26:17-30.

LESSON 2: WATCH AND PRAY

Lesson Aim: To help senior highers experience a close relationship with God through prayer.

Bible Basis: Psalm 69 and Matthew 26:36-46.

LESSON 3: THE CROSS

Lesson Aim: To help senior highers learn how Jesus' death on the cross provides a way to forgiveness.

Bible Basis: Psalm 22 and Matthew 27:32-56.

LESSON 4: THE PROMISED SURPRISE

Lesson Aim: To help senior highers understand how to live each day with Resurrection joy.

Bible Basis: Matthew 28:1-10.

PUBLICITY PAGE

Grab your senior highers' attention! Copy this page, then cut and paste the art of your choice in your church bulletin or newsletter to advertise this course on *Jesus' Death & Resurrection*. Or copy and use the ready-made flier as a bulletin insert.

Permission to photocopy clip art is granted for local church use.

Splash this art on posters, fliers or even postcards! Just add the vital details: the date and time the course begins, and where you'll meet.

It's that simple.

Come to _____

On _____

At _____

Come celebrate the joy of Jesus' Resurrection!

JESUS' DEATH & RESURRECTION

A 4-week high school course on the significance and importance of Jesus' Resurrection

A MEAL TO REMEMBER

To teenagers, the Lord's Supper may be little more than a ritual performed on a regular basis. But by recognizing the history of the Lord's Supper, and where the Passover meal originated, kids can understand the significance of the meal and learn to count on God's promises.

LESSON AIM

To help senior highers discover and remember God's promises.

OBJECTIVES

Students will:
● explore the history of the Passover meal;
● discover the similarities between the Passover meal and the Last Supper;
● experience a meal of remembering; and
● commit to remembering God's promises every day.

BIBLE BASIS
EXODUS 12:1-30
MATTHEW 26:17-30

Look up the following scriptures. Then read the background paragraphs to see how the passages relate to your senior highers.

In **Exodus 12:1-30**, the Israelites celebrate the Passover. After more than 400 years of bondage in Egypt, God freed the Israelites to go to the Promised Land. In order to remember God's fulfilled promise of deliverance, God told the Israelites to celebrate the Passover meal. This meal reminded the people how God instructed them to mark their doors with blood, so he would "pass over" them and not kill their firstborn—as he did with the Egyptians. This tradition was then passed from generation to generation.

The Passover meal is a significant reminder of God's fulfilled promises. Senior highers can be comforted and challenged by this memory of God's faithfulness—comforted because God kept his word and challenged because God's promise requires them to commit their lives to him.

In **Matthew 26:17-30**, Jesus shares the Passover meal with his disciples.

In this passage, Jesus creates a new covenant—a new meal to remember. Again, God's people are reminded he keeps his promises. This time the promise is that the Messiah (Jesus) would bear the people's sins. And this new promise frees God's people from the bondage of sin. Jesus tells his disciples to always remember God's faithfulness and live in his presence every day.

The Lord's Supper may be nothing more than a ritual to some senior highers. Though they may understand the reason for the supper, they may not fully understand the significance of the event. This passage reminds senior highers of the reason for the supper in the first place—and of God's faithfulness. The Lord's Supper can then become a way to shape and strengthen kids' faith.

THIS LESSON AT A GLANCE

Section	Minutes	What Students Will Do	Supplies
Opener (Option 1) (Option 2)	up to 5	**Best Meal Ever**—Describe the best meal they've ever had. **Thanksgiving Memory**—Write what they remember about their most recent Thanksgiving meal.	Paper plates, markers, paper, pencils, prize
Action and Reflection	15 to 20	**A Meal to Remember**—Enjoy a "meal" to celebrate friendship.	Crackers, cheese, orange juice, serving tray, cups
Bible Application	10 to 15	**Two Great Meals**—Examine the relationship between the Passover meal and the Last Supper.	"Meal to Remember" handouts (p. 18), markers, Bibles, bread, butter
Commitment	10 to 15	**Living in God's Promise**—Commit to remember God's promises every day.	Posterboard, markers, tape, paper, pencils
Closing (Option 1) (Option 2)	up to 5	**Blessings**—Write mealtime prayers, thanking God for keeping his promises. **Supper's Never Over**—Create human sculptures to represent how the Last Supper makes them feel.	Paper napkins, markers

The Lesson

☐ OPTION 1: BEST MEAL EVER

Give kids each a paper plate, a marker, a sheet of paper and a pencil. Have kids write on their plate the best meal they've ever had. Encourage kids to be as specific as possible in their description of the meal. Have kids describe the setting, atmosphere and menu. Then have kids each write their name on their plate and hand it to you.

Shuffle the plates and number them. Have kids number their papers according to the number of paper plates. Then read aloud a description and its number from one of the plates, and have kids each write on their paper their guess of who wrote the description. Read each description and its number, and have kids each write guesses for each on their paper.

After kids each have written their guesses for all the descriptions, read aloud each description and have kids call out their guesses. Then tell who wrote each description. Award a prize, such as a candy bar or a doughnut, to the person who had the most correct guesses on his or her paper.

Ask:

● **Was it easy to remember your best meal? Explain.** (No, I've had lots of good meals; yes, I have a good memory when it comes to food.)

● **What feelings did you have at that meal?** (I felt great; I was hungry; I was happy.)

● **What circumstances prompted those feelings?** (My family was all together; I was hungry; my favorite food was being served.)

● **Why are meals often associated with significant times in people's lives?** (Because food is important; because meals are part of celebrations.)

Say: **Today we're going to begin our course on Jesus' death and Resurrection by examining an important meal that reminds us of a significant event in Jesus' life.**

☐ OPTION 2: THANKSGIVING MEMORY

Form groups of no more than four. Say: **Thanksgiving is often a time of wonderful meals and fun family time. Think back to last Thanksgiving. In your group, describe the positive things you can remember about the holiday. Be specific in your descriptions and be sure to describe what you liked best about the meal.**

Give kids three or four minutes to discuss their Thanksgiving experiences.

Ask:

● **Was it easy to remember your last Thanksgiving? Ex-**

plain. (Yes, I always remember times when we have food; no, we don't do anything special on that day.)

● **What makes holidays such as Thanksgiving so full of meaning?** (They remind us of historical events; they bring families together.)

Say: **Today we're going to discover the significance of a meal Jesus had with his disciples. We all know the meal as the Last Supper, but it was more than simply a meal with friends.**

A MEAL TO REMEMBER

Note: Before this activity, prepare a meal of crackers, cheese and orange juice, and place it in another room. Place the crackers and cheese on a serving tray in the middle of the room. Have the juice already poured into cups.

Say: **I'd like to share a simple meal with you to celebrate our friendship. As soon as we leave this room, I'd like everyone to have an attitude of love and support for each other. Whenever we talk during the meal, be positive and supportive of each other. Say only uplifting things about each other. We'll come back in a few minutes to talk about our experience.**

Lead kids to the meal room. Before the meal, offer a prayer thanking God for bringing everyone together in this class. Then have kids serve each other crackers, cheese and orange juice.

Have kids each tell one positive memory they have of doing something with someone else in the class. For example, kids might tell stories about spending time at a retreat or simply talking after school. Remind kids to be serious and positive during this time. If kids don't know each other well, have them talk about important times they've spent with other friends.

Say: **I'd like this simple meal to remind us of the importance of our friendships. From now on, whenever you eat crackers and cheese, remember this time and the importance of the friendships God has given us.**

Form a circle and have kids take turns saying at least one positive thing about the person on his or her left. For example, kids might say, "You're caring and concerned about others" or "You're a great friend."

Then lead kids back to the regular meeting room.
Ask:

● **How'd you feel in the other room?** (Uncomfortable; great; nervous.)

● **Why is it important to celebrate our friendships?** (So we can remain friends; so we grow as friends; so we can learn the importance of friendships.)

● **How does the experience of going away to another room for this meal add to the experience?** (It helps us focus on the intent of the class; it separates the meal from the regular class.)

● **How is remembering our friendship when we eat crackers and cheese like remembering Jesus' life when we share in the Lord's Supper?** (We think back to the first time we shared the food and we remember the message; we're reminded of the ongoing importance of what's being celebrated.)

Say: **In Old Testament times, the Israelites celebrated the Passover as a reminder of God's faithfulness in getting them out of Egypt. In a similar manner, our meal serves as a reminder of an important aspect of our lives—friendship. When Jesus shared the Passover meal with his disciples just before his Crucifixion, the meal took on a new significance. Let's take a look at what that significance was.**

TWO GREAT MEALS

Form two groups. Give each group a "Meal to Remember" handout (p. 18), a marker and Bibles. Assign one of the following passages to each group: Exodus 12:1-30 or Matthew 26:17-30.

Say: **In your group, read the assigned passage and discuss the significance of the meal described in the passage. Then complete your handout based on what you discover.**

After six minutes, call time. Have the Exodus group describe its findings as you give each student a piece of bread to symbolize the meal. Tell kids not to eat the bread. Then have the Matthew group describe its findings as you go around and butter each person's bread. Once again, remind kids not to eat the bread yet.

Ask:

● **What are the similarities between these meals?** (Both are to remember important events; they're the same—both are the Passover meal.)

● **What are the differences between these meals?** (The meal with Jesus added a new thing to remember—Jesus' sacrifice; the Passover was started in the Exodus passage, it was simply being repeated in Matthew.)

● **How is the relationship between the bread and the butter like the relationship between the meals they represent?** (Butter improves the bread just as the Last Supper improves on the Passover meal; just as the butter was added to the bread, Jesus added new significance to the Passover meal.)

● **How was the meal we experienced earlier like the**

meals you just read about? (It was a meal to remind us of something important; it was shared by close friends.)

● **How does the Passover meal in Exodus represent a fulfillment of God's promise?** (It was a reminder that God delivered the Israelites.)

● **How does the Last Supper in Matthew represent a fulfillment of God's promise?** (It identifies Jesus as the Messiah who came to die for people's sins.)

● **How is Jesus the fulfillment of God's promise?** (He was sent to die for our sins; he showed us how to have a relationship with God.)

Say: **Just as the Passover meal was meant to remind the Israelites of God's fulfillment of his promises, the Lord's Supper is a reminder of God's fulfillment of his promise to free people from sin.**

Tell kids they can eat the bread and butter.

COMMITMENT
(10 to 15 minutes)

LIVING IN GOD'S PROMISE

Form groups of no more than four. Have kids talk about what it would've been like to be with Jesus at the Last Supper. Bring groups to the posterboard, one at a time, and have kids each write or draw something to represent how they'll remember God's promises every day. For example, someone might draw a rainbow or write a poem about God's faithfulness.

After kids each have contributed to the poster, have kids gather in a circle. Tape the posterboard to the wall and say: **This poster identifies our specific commitments to remember God's promises each day. Just as the Passover meal and the Last Supper represented people's remembrance of God's promises, let's be reminded of his promises every time we look at this poster.**

Give kids each a sheet of paper and a pencil. Say: **Remembering the significance of the Last Supper is important. But how does remembering God's promises help us in our everyday situations? On your paper, write one difficult situation you or a friend has faced recently.**

Collect the papers. Then have volunteers read the situations one at a time. After each situation is read, have kids brainstorm ways they can count on God's promises in that situation. For a situation about someone who gets picked on in school, responses might include: "God has promised to take care of us, even when things are bad" or "God will keep you strong when others try to tear you down."

Keep the poster in the room to remind kids of God's fulfillment of his promises through Jesus Christ.

Table Talk

The Table Talk activity in this course helps senior highers and their parents discuss the significance of Jesus' death and Resurrection.

If you choose to use the Table Talk activity, this is a good time to show students the "Table Talk" handout (p. 19). Ask them to spend time with their parents completing it.

Before kids leave, give them each the "Table Talk" handout to take home, or tell them you'll be sending it to their parents.

Or use the Table Talk idea found in the Bonus Ideas (p. 46) for a meeting based on the handout.

☐ OPTION 1: BLESSINGS

Give kids each a paper napkin and a marker. Have them each write on the napkin a mealtime prayer. Encourage kids to thank God for keeping his promises. Then close the meeting by having kids each read their prayer aloud for the rest of the group. Have kids each take their napkin home and read the prayer at the next family meal.

☐ OPTION 2: SUPPER'S NEVER OVER

Say: **The Last Supper was an important event in the disciples' lives. But the Last Supper's impact didn't end with the final sip of wine or the last piece of bread. When we understand the significance of the meal, we may feel excited, sad, or a mixture of both. For our closing today, form a human sculpture to represent how the Last Supper makes you feel. When everyone is frozen into a sculpture, I'll close with prayer.**

Join the group in creating human sculptures. Kids might kneel in prayer to symbolize their reverence or stand with arms open wide to symbolize their acceptance of the Last Supper. Then close with prayer, thanking God for keeping his promises and sending Jesus to die for each person.

CLOSING
(up to 5 minutes)

If You Still Have Time . . .

Lord's Supper Discussion—Have a pastor visit the class to discuss your denomination's understanding of the Lord's Supper. Encourage kids to ask questions about the meaning and process of the Lord's Supper in your church.

The Drama of the Last Supper—Have kids act out Matthew 26:17-30 as a drama. Assign parts to be played; then walk through the drama, using scripture as a guide. Afterward, have kids talk about how they felt in the various roles.

Meal to Remember

Read your scripture. Then answer the following questions in your group:

● What's the reason for the meal?

● What are the circumstances surrounding the meal?

● What impact does the meal have on people's faith?

● What can we learn from this meal to help us grow as Christians?

● If you'd been there, what would you remember most about this meal?

Table Talk

To the Parent: We're involved in a senior high course at church called *Jesus' Death & Resurrection*. Students are exploring the significance of events leading up to and following Jesus' death on the cross. We'd like you and your teenager to discuss this important topic. Use this page to help you do that.

Parent and senior higher

Take turns answering the following questions:
- If you only had 10 words to summarize your faith, what would you say?
- What is the significance of Jesus' death and Resurrection?
- Why is it important to remember Jesus' death and Resurrection?
- How can you share your Resurrection joy with someone else?

Describe a time your love for someone took you through sacrifice or struggles. Discuss how you felt and talk about how this is like or unlike Jesus' feelings as he suffered on the cross.

Complete the following sentences:
- To me, the Lord's Supper means . . .
- I think prayer is important because . . .
- One time I felt especially close to God was . . .
- A time I really celebrated my faith was . . .
- The greatest expression of love is . . .
- The Easter season is important to me because . . .
- When I think of Jesus' death and Resurrection, I feel . . .

Together, read John 3:16-18 and John 15:12-15. How is the story of Jesus' death and Resurrection a symbol of God's great love for us?

LESSON 2

WATCH AND PRAY

Teenagers are used to doing things quickly. They catch the latest world news with the press of a button on a remote control unit; cook up a batch of microwave popcorn in minutes; and have pizza delivered in 30 minutes or less. But kids need "slow down" time too. When kids learn to slow down and spend time in prayer, they can be refreshed to take on another day of busy schedules with renewed energy.

LESSON AIM

To help senior highers experience a close relationship with God through prayer.

OBJECTIVES

Students will:
- explore the importance of prayer;
- experience a time of prayer;
- learn how to be alone with God; and
- examine Jesus' struggle in Gethsemane and the strength he received from prayer.

BIBLE BASIS
PSALM 69
MATTHEW 26:36-46

Look up the following scriptures. Then read the background paragraphs to see how the passages relate to your senior highers.

In **Psalm 69**, the Psalmist cries out for God to save him.

In this Psalm, the Psalmist is feeling totally abandoned and surrounded by enemies. Wherever he turns for comfort no one is there. He describes the pain and suffering vividly. Yet even in this moment of agony, he still has his relationship with God. Prayer keeps him connected to his source of help.

Life is filled with ups and downs for most teenagers. "One day you walk in grace; the next, you trip and fall on your face" is an appropriate description for kids. They often feel crushed and abandoned. Like the Psalmist, teenagers may feel lost. But they also can feel comfort, knowing they have a connection with God through prayer.

In **Matthew 26:36-46**, Jesus prays in the Garden of Gethsemane.

It's clear from this passage that Jesus is fully aware of the upcoming events. He knows he must endure great pain in a single act of sacrifice—his death. But, like the Psalmist, he feels abandoned—with God alone to talk to. In this passage, we see the incredible power of prayer—of our connection with God.

Teenagers can feel confident in their faith, knowing God understands the pain of being crushed and abandoned. And they can learn the importance of a direct connection with God through prayer. They can learn to watch and pray.

THIS LESSON AT A GLANCE

Section	Minutes	What Students Will Do	Supplies
Opener (Option 1)	up to 5	**Prayer Partners**—Play a game to find prayer partners.	"Prayer Partners" handouts (p. 28), scissors, blindfolds
(Option 2)		**Four Corners**—Form groups based on how they answer questions about prayer.	Paper, marker, tape
Action and Reflection	10 to 15	**Alone With God**—Pray in gradually shrinking groups until they're alone with God.	Black plastic sheets (optional), tape (optional)
Bible Application	10 to 15	**Gethsemane**—Act out Matthew 26:36-46 and discuss Jesus' prayer time in Gethsemane.	Bibles
Commitment	10 to 15	**Prayer Vigil**—Plan and design a time of prayer.	"Prayer Plans" handouts (p. 29), pencils
Closing (Option 1)	5 to 10	**Prayer Chain**—List prayer concerns, and tape them together to make a "prayer chain."	Paper strips, pencils, tape
(Option 2)		**Prayer Song**—Write prayer lyrics to a familiar song.	Songbooks or hymnals, paper, pencils

The Lesson

OPENER

(up to 5 minutes)

☐ OPTION 1: PRAYER PARTNERS

Copy and cut apart the strips from the "Prayer Partners" handout (p. 28). Give kids each one strip and tell them to read it silently. Be sure you distribute at least two of each strip you use. If your group is smaller than 12, use only a few "Prayer Partner" strips—at least two of each.

Say: **In a moment, I'll blindfold each of you. Your job during this activity is to pray about today's lesson according to the instructions on your strip. Keep praying and try to find a partner (or partners) who's praying the same way. You may not tell anyone what your strip says; you'll have to find your partner simply by listening to people's prayers. When you think you've found a match, don't say anything; just join hands and hold up your hands together. I'll come around and check your strips. If you've found your partner, I'll let you take off your blindfolds. If not, keep trying.**

Remind kids that prayer doesn't have to always be "heavy" but should be taken seriously. If kids laugh during this activity, briefly discuss why they laughed. Kids may simply be enjoying the activity—that's great!

After kids each find their partner, form a circle.

Ask:

● **What does this activity tell us about prayer?** (People pray in different ways; some prayers are loud and obnoxious.)

● **How easy was it to find your partner?** (Easy; difficult.)

● **How was your search for your partner like searching for answers from God when you're struggling with problems?** (Sometimes you find an answer right away; sometimes you can't find your answer; sometimes your answer is right in front of you and you don't see it.)

● **What's the power of prayer?** (It can help answer problems; it can give you strength in tough times; it can calm you.)

Say: **Today we're going to examine a very powerful prayer time in Jesus' life to better understand the power of prayer for each of us.**

☐ OPTION 2: FOUR CORNERS

Use paper and a marker to make four signs, each with one of the following letters on it: "A," "B," "C" or "D." Tape signs each in a different corner of the room.

Have kids look around at the placement of the signs. Say: **I'm going to read statements about prayer. For each, I'll read four options. As I read the options, decide which one** describes you best. Then move to the letter associated with that option. For each item, look around at the way other people answered. Don't judge people by their answers, just observe what happens.

Read aloud the following options, allowing time for kids to move to the appropriate corners:

1. The amount of time I usually spend in prayer each day is . . .
(a) 0 to 5 minutes.
(b) 6 to 30 minutes.
(c) 30 minutes or more.
(d) private—I'd rather not say.
2. The place I pray most is . . .
(a) at school.
(b) in my room.
(c) at church.
(d) somewhere else.
3. My major prayer concerns are . . .
(a) related to world issues.
(b) related to personal problems.
(c) related to friends' problems.
(d) related to community problems.
4. My favorite position for praying is . . .
(a) kneeling.
(b) standing.
(c) sitting.
(d) lying down.
5. When it comes to praying, I prefer to . . .
(a) write prayers on paper.
(b) read written prayers.
(c) pray silently.
(d) pray aloud.
6. The hardest thing about praying is . . .
(a) making time to pray.
(b) making up my own prayers.
(c) praying for people I don't like.
(d) praying for myself.

After kids respond to the last item, have them form a circle. Ask:

● **What'd you notice about this activity?** (People have different prayer habits; we all have similar approaches to prayer.)

● **What's most important about prayer?** (Spending time in prayer; your attitude; what you say.)

Say: **Prayer was a key element in Jesus' life. When he faced the most difficult time in his life—just before his Crucifixion—Jesus spent time in prayer. Today we're going to take a look at that important time with God.**

If you sent the "Table Talk" handout (p. 19) to parents last week, discuss students' reactions to the activity. Ask volunteers to share what they learned from the discussion with their parents.

ACTION AND REFLECTION
(10 to 15 minutes)

ALONE WITH GOD

For this activity, you'll need to be able to make the room as dark as possible. If necessary, tape black plastic over windows to cover light that enters the room. Or meet in a room that's easily darkened.

Begin this activity with kids in a circle and the lights on. Have volunteers pray, asking God to help the class learn more about the power of prayer. If kids haven't prayed much before, briefly describe how prayer is simply communicating with God. You may want to give them an example of a simple prayer. After a minute or so, form two groups and separate them in the room. Have groups each continue to pray about any topics they like. After another minute, divide the two groups into four groups and separate them in the room. Continue to shrink the size of the groups until each person is sitting by him- or herself in the room. Then turn out the lights.

Say: **In silence, continue your prayers. But now it's just you and God. Take the next three minutes to talk with God silently—and let him talk to you.**

Kids will probably get uncomfortable about praying for three minutes in silence. That's okay. You'll discuss their feelings when time is up.

After three minutes (with the lights still off and kids still by themselves), ask:

● **How does it feel to be alone with God?** (Uncomfortable; strange; comforting.)

● **How do the prayer times with other group members compare to your quiet time alone?** (I like the group prayers better; I feel more comfortable with God alone.)

● **What do your feelings when alone say about your relationship with God?** (If you're uncomfortable alone with God you might need to work on your relationship with him; if you feel good when alone with God, your relationship is probably good.)

● **Why is time alone with God important?** (Because it refreshes us; because it helps us grow in faith; because it's our communication with God.)

Say: **Before Jesus was crucified, he went to a place called Gethsemane with his disciples. But his disciples couldn't stay awake while Jesus prayed, because they were tired. Unlike Jesus, the disciples didn't fully comprehend the importance of prayer in this time of great trial. Yet this time Jesus spent alone with God paints a great picture of the importance and power of prayer.**

GETHSEMANE

Have volunteers act out Matthew 26:36-46. You'll need a person to play Jesus and others to play the parts of the disciples. Read the story aloud as kids act it out.

Ask:

● **How do you think Jesus felt in this situation?** (Frustrated; upset; anxious.)

● **Why'd Jesus want his disciples to stay awake with him?** (He wanted company; he was overwhelmed with sadness and wanted their support.)

● **How is Jesus' time alone with God like or unlike the time you spent alone with God in the previous activity?** (God was listening to each prayer; Jesus was in a crisis situation, we weren't; time alone with God is energizing.)

● **What did Jesus gain from his prayer time with God?** (Strength to keep going; confidence; comfort; a challenge to move forward.)

● **What can we gain from our prayer times with God?** (Strength; confidence; comfort.)

● **What benefits does prayer have for you?** (It gives me answers to problems; it makes me feel close to God; it strengthens my faith.)

Form groups of no more than five. Give groups each a Bible. Say: **Have someone in your group read aloud Psalm 69. After reading the Psalm, talk about how it made you feel. Then, one at a time, describe a time you felt lost or abandoned and how you were able to get beyond your feeling of loneliness.**

After kids finish sharing their stories, say: **You may feel frustrated or scared—just as Jesus was—as you face trials in your life. But God is always near—you can reach out to him in prayer, no matter what situation you're in.**

PRAYER VIGIL

BIBLE APPLICATION
(10 to 15 minutes)

COMMITMENT
(10 to 15 minutes)

Note: Some or many of your teenagers may never have experienced an extended prayer time or a "prayer vigil." Extended prayer times may make kids uncomfortable, but kids will begin to understand the importance and power of prayer.

You may want to suggest next week's lesson time for the prayer vigil—extending this course to five weeks. Discuss this activity with your senior pastor before announcing it to your kids. He or she may have good advice on how to present the idea to your kids according to your denominational beliefs.

Form groups of no more than five. Give groups each a "Prayer Plans" handout (p. 29) and a pencil. Say: **Jesus knew the power of prayer. In his long night in Gethsemane, Jesus struggled with his fears about the future—and was** comforted by his father's answer to his prayer. We, too, can count on God to help us in times of need.

In your group, complete the handout and brainstorm a specific plan for spending an extended time (more than 30 minutes) in prayer with others. Make your plan as practical as possible and be sure to include how you'll coordinate the plan. In a few minutes, we'll regroup and discuss the plans each group has created. We'll be putting the best plan into action in the coming weeks.

Give groups seven minutes to work on their plans. Then have groups each explain their plan to the rest of the group. Have kids discuss the plan they feel most comfortable committing to. If plans end up with very little prayer time, challenge kids to think about which plan Jesus might choose. Then have kids offer suggestions for fine-tuning the winning plan.

Ask for volunteers to take charge of the prayer vigil. Ask kids to each sign the back of the chosen plan as a sign of their commitment to make it work.

Then form a circle. Say: **Together, we can make this event work. Each of us brings a unique skill or ability to help make this prayer vigil successful.**

Have kids each say one positive thing about the person on their left, describing traits or abilities that person has that can make the prayer vigil a success. For example, kids might say, "Your organizing skill will help this event work" or "Your good ideas helped us make a good plan."

Be supportive during the coming week as kids plan this event.

CLOSING
(5 to 10 minutes)

☐ OPTION 1: PRAYER CHAIN

Give kids each a 1×6-inch paper strip and a pencil. Say: **Prayer is our connection with God. Take a moment to consider what you'd like to talk with God about. You may have a concern you'd like to pray for or a joy you'd like to thank God for.**

Have kids each write on their slip a prayer request or something they're thankful for. For example, kids might write concerns about family situations or joys about things that are going well.

Have a volunteer read aloud his or her strip, then tape the ends together to make a paper chain link. As kids each read aloud their prayer request, have them each add their strip to the previous links to form a "prayer chain." Connect the ends of the chain together to form a complete circle with the paper links.

Have kids form a circle. In closing, pass the prayer chain around the circle and have kids each offer a silent prayer as they hold the chain. Remind kids about their commitment to the prayer vigil.

☐ OPTION 2: PRAYER SONG

Form groups of no more than five. Give groups each a songbook or hymnal, paper and pencils. Have groups each write new words for a verse or chorus of a familiar song using the theme of prayer.

Give groups five minutes to write their verse or chorus. Then have groups each sing their verse or chorus as a closing prayer for the lesson. Remind kids about their commitment to the prayer vigil.

If You Still Have Time . . .

Everyday Prayer—Have kids discuss ways they can pray in everyday situations. Include a discussion of ways to pray at school, home and while working or playing. Ask kids what it means to have an attitude of prayer.

Prayer Mural—Tape a few sheets of newsprint to the wall, and have kids each write or draw something on the newsprint to represent prayer. Kids might write short prayers, draw pictures symbolizing prayer or describe the benefits of prayers. Keep the mural up for a few weeks to remind kids of the importance of prayer.

PRAYER PARTNERS

Copy this box and cut apart the strips of paper along the dotted lines.

Pray in a quiet voice. Don't draw attention to yourself.

Use lots of gestures and speak boldly as you pray.

Use old English language in your prayer. For example, instead of "you," say "thee" and instead of "help," say "helpeth."

Pray with your hands folded and your face lifted to the sky. In your prayer, describe your sense of wonder at God's great love.

Pray silently.

Pray on your knees. You'll need to scoot around on the floor to find your partner.

Pray in a quiet voice. Don't draw attention to yourself.

Use lots of gestures and speak boldly as you pray.

Use old English language in your prayer. For example, instead of "you," say "thee" and instead of "help," say "helpeth."

Pray with your hands folded and your face lifted to the sky. In your prayer, describe your sense of wonder at God's great love.

Pray silently.

Pray on your knees. You'll need to scoot around on the floor to find your partner.

PRAYER PLANS

Answer the questions on this handout to help you prepare a plan for a time of extended prayer. Then describe your plan in detail in the space provided.

● What would you like to accomplish with an extended prayer time or "prayer vigil"?

● Who would you like to have involved in your prayer vigil? senior highers? the whole congregation? the community?

● Where would you hold this event?

● How would you advertise the prayer vigil?

● How long would the prayer time last?

● How would you structure the prayer time? (Do you pray for specific things or requests during certain hours?)

● Would you include singing or scripture-reading during the prayer time? Explain.

● What else might you include?

Based on your answers to the above questions, complete the following plan for your prayer vigil:

Date:

Time:

Place:

Length of prayer vigil:

Description of event:

LESSON 3

THE CROSS

Jesus' death on the cross can be a source of power for teenagers. By understanding Jesus' agony on the cross, kids can begin to see the incredible sacrifice Jesus made. And by understanding Jesus' sacrifice, kids can draw on the power of God's forgiveness for their sins—and learn to forgive others as they've been forgiven.

LESSON AIM

To help senior highers learn how Jesus' death on the cross provides a way to forgiveness.

OBJECTIVES

Students will:
● explore how God sees sin;
● examine the Crucifixion from a first-person perspective;
● discover Jesus' agony on the cross; and
● commit to forgive others as Jesus has forgiven them.

BIBLE BASIS
PSALM 22
MATTHEW 27:32-56

Look up the following scriptures. Then read the background paragraphs to see how the passages relate to your senior highers.

In **Psalm 22**, the Psalmist cries out for God not to forsake him.

Jesus quoted Psalm 22 as he was crucified. The Psalmist's pain and suffering is the ultimate agony of feeling abandoned, despised, insulted and scorned. Jesus must've felt all this and more as he contemplated God's will for him and the cross he faced.

High school students have felt the pain of being mocked, insulted and jeered at. They, like the Psalmist, probably question whether standing up for their faith is worth the pain. They may wonder: Is my faith a source of power or a stumbling block?

In **Matthew 27:32-56**, Jesus' Crucifixion is described.

In this passage, we learn about God's great act of reconciliation as he reaches out to humankind through Jesus' death. By

Jesus' death on the cross, God showed how painful it was for God to forgive—and how far he was willing to go to forgive us.

For teenagers to grow into close relationships with friends and family, forgiveness is essential. But to forgive and to be forgiven takes a lot of strength. Kids can learn to draw power from the greatest act of forgiveness—Jesus' sacrifice on the cross.

THIS LESSON AT A GLANCE

Section	Minutes	What Students Will Do	Supplies
Opener (Option 1)	5 to 10	**Dividing Wall**—Build a wall and discover what divides people and God.	Boxes, newsprint, tape, markers
(Option 2)		**Divine Drama**—Create and perform skits based on Matthew 18:21-35.	Bibles
Action and Reflection	10 to 15	**The Pain**—Experience how God sees sin.	"My Life" handouts (p. 36), pencils, tape, markers
Bible Application	10 to 15	**And You Were There**—Examine the Crucifixion from a "first-person" perspective.	Five candles, matches, "At the Cross" handouts (p. 37)
Commitment	10 to 15	**Hammer and Nail**—Nail their sins to a cross and commit to forgive others as Jesus has forgiven them.	Two pieces of wood, hammer, nails, pencils, "My Life" handouts from The Pain, tape, Bible
Closing (Option 1)	up to 5	**Carrying the Cross**—Carry the cross to a "tomb."	The cross from Hammer and Nail
(Option 2)		**Silent Reflection**—Pray silently around the cross.	

The Lesson

OPTION 1: DIVIDING WALL

Place a bunch of boxes (at least 20 of various sizes), newsprint and tape in the center of the room. Form two groups and have each stay on one side of an imaginary line in the middle of the room. Say: **Take the next five minutes to build a wall down the center of the room. Make it as tall and wide as you can, using these supplies. You may work together on the wall, but you may not communicate with the people on the other side of the wall. You must stay on**

OPENER
(5 to 10 minutes)

your side of the "line" where the wall will be built.

After a couple of minutes, call time. Give each kid a marker. Have them each write on their side of the wall things that build walls between them and God, such as lying, bad language or deception.

Then have groups switch sides and read the other group's wall. Ask:

● **How'd you feel as you were building the wall?** (Great; uncomfortable; confused.)

● **How is building this wall like building walls between you and God?** (The wall keeps us apart; it may seem fun sometimes to build walls; walls are often too easy to build.)

Say: **When Jesus faced his own death on the cross, he probably felt as if people had built a wall between them and him. He felt alone. But his death on the cross was the greatest wall-breaker ever. By dying on the cross, Jesus forgave our sins and broke down the walls we'd built separating us from God.**

Have kids break down the wall.

Say: **Look around. Some of you may see a bunch of blocks people might trip on. And some of you may see the blocks and remember the wall being broken by a great power. Jesus' death on the cross can also be viewed as a stumbling block or a source of power. Today we'll explore Jesus' Crucifixion and see what it means for each of us.**

☐ OPTION 2: DIVINE DRAMA

Form groups of no more than five. Give groups each a Bible. Have them each read aloud Matthew 18:21-35, then create a short skit dramatizing the passage (either in the biblical setting or updated to a modern setting). Give groups five minutes to create their skits.

Have groups each perform their skit.

Then ask:

● **What do these skits tell us about the importance of forgiveness?** (How we forgive others is how God will forgive us; forgiveness should be given no matter what was done wrong.)

Say: **Jesus taught forgiveness, but he also performed the ultimate act of forgiveness by dying on the cross for us. Today we'll take a close look at Jesus' Crucifixion and what it means.**

ACTION AND REFLECTION
(10 to 15 minutes)

THE PAIN

This lesson includes activities that may make your kids feel uncomfortable. Be prepared for kids' responses to the lesson. Some may giggle or laugh to release tension, others may cry during one of the activities. Be sure to talk about how kids are feeling throughout the lesson. This may be an appropriate lesson to share the message of Christ with non-Christians in your class.

Give kids each a "My Life" handout (p. 36) and a pencil. Have kids each complete their handout.

Afterward, have kids tape the handouts to the wall. Give each teenager a marker.

Say: **These papers represent who you are. For this next activity, we'll imagine these papers *are* you.**

On "go," use the markers to deface your own handout. You may write derogatory names such as "Bible baby" or "Holy roller" on the sheets, but don't use profanity. You may even tear the papers if you want. When I call time, stop defacing the papers and step back from the wall.

Give kids a minute or two to deface the handouts. Then call time. Have kids collect their papers and sit in a circle.

Ask:

● **How do you feel as you look at your paper?** (Angry; upset; sad.)

● **How is that like the way God feels when he sees our sins?** (He's sad; it makes God angry.)

● **How'd you feel as you defaced your paper?** (Angry; uncomfortable.)

● **In what ways do we sometimes deface Jesus' name?** (By lying; by not spending enough time in prayer; by swearing.)

● **Who were the people who "defaced" Jesus at the time of his Crucifixion?** (The Roman soldiers; the Jews; everyone.)

● **Look at your paper. How does the way it looks reflect what sin does to our lives?** (Sin tears us apart; sin hurts us; we all sin.)

Say: **Just as we may've felt bad about the ruined papers, God must feel bad about the sin in people's lives. He wanted to reconcile the world to himself, so he sent a sinless man, Jesus to die for our sins. Though we deserved to die, Jesus died in our place. Jesus' agony on the cross was probably much more than physical pain. He knew he shouldered the sins of the world as he hung from the cross.**

AND YOU WERE THERE

Place five candles in a circle. Light them and turn out the lights. Give kids each an "At the Cross" handout (p. 37). Say: **This handout contains a short readers theater play based on Jesus' Crucifixion. Follow the instructions and read together when your part comes up. Remember to make this a serious time—imagine you're actually at Jesus' Crucifixion as you read your part.**

Read the narrator's part and have kids follow along, reading the guys' or girls' parts as appropriate. Kids will have to stay close to the candles to read their scripts. As the script is read, blow out one candle every time you see a small candle on the script. Just after reading the last section, blow out the final candle and remain silent for a moment.

Then turn on the lights and have someone read aloud Matthew 27:32-56.

**BIBLE
APPLICATION**
(10 to 15 minutes)

Ask:
- **How'd you feel as you read the script?** (Uncomfortable; sad; angry.)
- **What do the play and the scripture passage tell us about Jesus' death on the cross?** (It was a powerful event; it was a painful time for Jesus.)
- **How might Jesus' death be a stumbling block for some people?** (They wonder why he had to die; they don't believe he rose again.)
- **How might Jesus' death be a source of power for people?** (His death allows us to reach God; his death forgave our sins; by his death we're freed from sin.)
- **Why is Jesus' death on the cross important?** (Because only God's son could die for our sins; if he didn't die, our sins wouldn't be forgiven; since he didn't have any sins, his death took away our sins.)

Say: **Jesus' death on the cross was God's great act of forgiveness. And that message of forgiveness should remind us to follow in Jesus' example and forgive others as he forgave us.**

COMMITMENT
(10 to 15 minutes)

HAMMER AND NAIL

Note: You'll need two pieces of wood for this activity—2×4s work best. Make one board 5 feet long and the other 3 feet long. If you don't have boards, do this activity with a cardboard cross and have kids tape their papers to the cross.

Silently nail the two pieces of wood together to form a cross. Dim the lights or use candlelight for this activity.

Say: **When Jesus died on the cross, he took our sins with him. I'm going to give each of you a pencil. On the back of your "My Life" handout, write key words to describe areas in your life where you need God's forgiveness. You don't need to describe these areas specifically, just use a word or two you'll recognize. In a few minutes, we'll nail these papers to a wooden cross. Work silently, and then come up one at a time when you're done. While others are coming up to the cross, use the time for personal reflection and prayer. Listen to the hammering and think about Jesus' sacrifice for you.**

Distribute pencils to kids. Some kids might need tape to put their handouts back together. After you've completed your handout, go up to the cross and use a nail to attach the handout to the cross. Help direct kids who come up after you.

When everyone has nailed his or her paper to the cross, read aloud Psalm 22. Say: **God has not abandoned us, but we've abandoned him by our sin. Let us ask his forgive-**

ness for times when we've "defaced" God.

Form pairs. Have partners each verbally commit to seeking God's forgiveness for sins they've committed. Then have them each commit to forgive others as Jesus has forgiven them.

Bring the group together in a circle around the cross. Say: **During the coming week, let's remember Jesus' sacrifice and the incredible love God has for each of us.**

Read aloud John 3:16. Use John 3:16 to affirm each teenager's importance to God. Go around the circle and have kids join you in repeating the verse, using each person's name in place of "the world." For example, as you come up to Micah, you'd say: "For God so loved Micah that he gave his one and only son that whoever believes in him shall not perish but have eternal life."

☐ OPTION 1: CARRYING THE CROSS

Have kids form a tight circle around the cross, pick up the cross and quietly carry it to a closet or a corner of the room that represents a tomb. Encourage kids to accept Jesus' death on the cross as forgiveness for their sins. Have volunteers close in prayer.

After kids leave, collect the handouts they nailed to the cross and throw them away. Hide the cross somewhere and save it until next week's lesson.

☐ OPTION 2: SILENT REFLECTION

Say: **Jesus' death on the cross was a powerful event. The whole world shuddered with his death. Yet by his death on the cross, we've all been given life. Our sins died on the cross with Jesus.**

Spend a moment or two in prayer around the cross. Thank God for sacrificing his son for you. And ask him to help you understand the importance of Jesus' death for your life. Then, when you've finished praying, leave the room silently.

After kids have all gone, hide the cross somewhere and save it for next week. Collect the handouts the students nailed to the cross and throw them away.

C L O S I N G
(up to 5 minutes)

If You Still Have Time . . .

Forgiveness Feelings—Form groups of no more than five. Have groups each discuss how they feel when forgiven or when forgiving others. Ask kids to tell about specific times they forgave someone or someone forgave them.

Hymns of the Cross—Sing a hymn about Jesus' Crucifixion, such as "O Sacred Head, Now Wounded," "The Old Rugged Cross" or "Were You There?" Afterward, ask kids what the hymn means to them. If your group doesn't like singing, play a recording of the hymn or have kids read the words.

My Life

Think of this handout as a picture of you. Complete the sections below to describe your life.

Name: _____

Complete the following sentences.

● Three unique things about me are . . .

● If I could do anything I wanted, I'd . . .

● If I were to describe myself to a stranger, I'd say . . .

● My life is . . .

Draw a self-portrait below.

AT THE CROSS

There are three different parts in this drama: Narrator, Guys and Girls. Read aloud your part in turn.

Narrator: At noon, the whole country was covered with darkness. The people watched as Jesus hung on the cross. Some were there out of curiosity. Some came to cry for him. Others came to mock him. Out of the darkness, Jesus cried aloud from the cross, "My God, my God, why have you forsaken me?"

Guys: What'd he say?

Girls: He's crying out for his God.

Narrator: People nearby tried to make Jesus drink some cheap wine. They took a sponge, soaked it in the wine, then held it out on a long stick to Jesus' lips.

Guys: Here, drink it. Drink it! It'll ease the pain.

Girls: Wait, let him suffer! Let's see if Elijah is coming to save him now.

Narrator: (a loud cry of Jesus' dying breath) "Ahhhhhh!" (pause) With one final cry, Jesus gave up his spirit. Suddenly the Earth shook. Graves opened and people who were buried came to life. Everywhere, people scattered in panic.

Girls: What's that? What's happening?

Guys: (frightened) It's an earthquake! Run!

Girls: What does this mean?

Guys: It's him! It's all because of Jesus.

Girls: It can't be. He's just a man . . . or could he be . . . ?

Guys: The son of God?

All: He was the son of God. Oh, how I wish I'd followed him.

Narrator: As evening came, Joseph of Arimathea took Jesus to a tomb and buried him.

LESSON 4

THE PROMISED SURPRISE

aster is more than a miraculous historical event—it's the source of power that allows Christians to live joyfully every day. Teenagers can learn to rely on the power of Jesus' Resurrection as they grow closer to God in their faith journey.

LESSON AIM

To help senior highers understand how to live each day with Resurrection joy.

OBJECTIVES

Students will:
● celebrate surprises;
● discover how Jesus' Resurrection was God's gracious surprise;
● learn to live with Resurrection joy each day; and
● celebrate their relationships with Christ.

BIBLE BASIS
MATTHEW 28:1-10

Look up the following scripture. Then read the background paragraphs to see how the passage relates to your senior highers.

In **Matthew 28:1-10**, Jesus appears to Mary Magdalene after his Resurrection.

This passage shows how Resurrection power can remove obstacles that seem immovable. Just as the stone was rolled away from Jesus' tomb, walls that separated us from God were removed by Jesus' Resurrection. The two women who went to Jesus' tomb were prepared to continue their mourning. But what a surprise! The stone was rolled away and Jesus was alive.

Teenagers can learn from this passage how God replaces emptiness with fullness of new life in God. An empty tomb means an opportunity for a full and abundant life. Jesus was able to overcome death and bring new life to all who believe in him.

Section	Minutes	What Students Will Do	Supplies
Opener (Option 1)	up to 5	**Jack-in-the-Box**—Be surprised by a jack-in-the-box.	Jack-in-the-box, wrapping paper, scissors, tape
(Option 2)		**Surprise Me**—Guess surprising things about each other.	3×5 cards, pencils
Action and Reflection	10 to 15	**Surprise!**—Experience being surprised and talk about Resurrection joy.	Balloons, streamers, confetti, the cross from Lesson 3, black plastic (optional), candle, matches, snackfoods
Bible Application	10 to 15	**Rolling the Stone Away**—Turn rocks into symbols of joy.	Bibles, large rocks, paint, paintbrushes
Commitment	10 to 15	**Joy Year Round**—Brainstorm practical ways to live with Resurrection joy every day.	"Joy Surprise" handouts (p. 44), pencils, tape, balloons from Surprise!, permanent marker
Closing (Option 1)	5 to 10	**Resurrection Joy**—Recite a responsive reading expressing joy.	"It's a Celebration!" handouts (p. 45), whistles, construction paper
(Option 2)		**Resurrection Reflection**—Quietly reflect on the meaning of Jesus' death and Resurrection.	Bedsheet, string

The Lesson

Note: Before the lesson, prepare a room (that can easily be darkened) for the Surprise! activity by decorating it with colorful balloons, streamers and confetti. Make the room as colorful as you can. If space is tight at your church, consider using a kitchen or basement room for this activity. Place the cross from Lesson 3 on the floor near the entrance to the room (be sure all the papers have been removed from the previous week's activity). Make sure all the lights are out and the room is very dark. Use black plastic to cover windows if necessary. Place snackfoods on a table in the room. Lock the door so kids don't wander into the room by accident. Use your regular meeting area to start the lesson. You'll move to this room during the Surprise! activity.

☐ OPTION 1: JACK-IN-THE-BOX

Wrap a jack-in-the-box like a Christmas or birthday gift, then turn it upside down. Carefully cut the wrapping paper, and tape it to the cover so "Jack" can pop out when you turn the crank. Be sure the crank is accessible.

O P E N E R
(up to 5 minutes)

When kids arrive, say: **I've got a surprise for you. This gift represents God's love for us. Let's turn the crank and see what happens.**

Turn the crank slowly. When Jack pops out of the bottom, watch kids' reactions.

Ask:

● **How'd you feel when Jack popped out of the bottom of the box instead of the top?** (Surprised; disappointed.)

● **How is this surprise like God's expression of love for us?** (God loves us in surprising ways; God surprised us with Jesus' Resurrection.)

Say: **This jack-in-the-box is like God's promise. His love sometimes surprises us. And the most wonderful surprise God gave us is something we can celebrate every day—Jesus' Resurrection.**

☐ OPTION 2: SURPRISE ME

Give kids each two 3×5 cards and a pencil. Say: **On each of your cards, list one thing about yourself that other people here probably don't know. You might list an award you've won or a famous relative. Try to surprise us with what you write.**

Collect the cards and shuffle them. Then read each card aloud, one at a time. Have kids guess who wrote each card. Then have kids each tell what they wrote.

Ask:

● **What surprised you most about what people wrote?**

● **How do you feel when you're surprised?** (Happy; embarrassed; confused.)

● **What things have you recently been surprised about?** (A friend took me out to eat; my mom bought me a new sweater; my dad cooked breakfast.)

● **How are these surprises like the surprises God gives us?** (You don't always know what's coming; God's surprises make us happy.)

Say: **We've all been surprised in one way or another. You may've been surprised about something a friend wrote on a card. Or you may've enjoyed a birthday surprise. But one of the greatest surprises of all is something we can celebrate every day—Jesus rose from the grave!**

ACTION AND REFLECTION
(10 to 15 minutes)

SURPRISE!

Say: **Last week, we experienced the pain of Jesus' death on the cross. For this next activity, we need to be serious and meditative. We're going to visit Jesus' tomb. When we leave this room, let's be quiet and reflect on the sacrifice Jesus made on the cross.**

Take kids silently to the room you prepared. Light a candle and walk into the room (keep the lights off). Place the candle near the cross and form a circle around the cross.

Say: **Jesus' death set us free from sin. Think about how difficult it must've been for Jesus to give his life for others—especially since many despised him.**

Have kids close their eyes and pray silently for 30 seconds. When time is up, blow out the candle, turn on the lights and yell: **Surprise!**

Say: **Jesus has risen from the dead! Let's celebrate!**

Have kids toss the balloons and streamers around the room in celebration. Encourage kids to enjoy the snackfoods.

Then have kids form a circle, and ask:

● **What were you thinking when I led you to this room?** (I wondered if you'd surprise us; I was thinking about Jesus' death on the cross.)

● **How was the surprise of this celebration like the surprise of Jesus' Resurrection?** (People were thrilled to know Jesus was alive; we can celebrate Jesus' Resurrection; both surprises made something sad into something glad.)

● **What's the greatest surprise that's ever happened to you?** (Winning a contest; having a surprise party thrown for me.)

● **What made Jesus' Resurrection a surprise?** (People didn't believe he'd rise from the dead; people just don't come alive after they've died.)

Say: **Last week, we attached to the cross papers that listed sins we needed forgiveness for. Today those papers are gone. As Jesus died on the cross, our sins died with him. By rising again, Jesus also conquered death and provided us a path to God. What a fantastic surprise!**

Give kids a couple of minutes to continue enjoying the snackfoods. Then have kids each collect a balloon and take it back to the regular meeting room. (They'll use the balloon during the Joy Year Round activity.)

ROLLING THE STONE AWAY

Form groups of no more than five. Read aloud Matthew 28:1-10.

Ask:

● **What happened in this passage?** (Jesus rose from the dead; two women went to see Jesus' body and were surprised.)

Have groups each form themselves into a human sculpture to show how they would've responded if they'd been with the women who found the open tomb. Have kids look around at other groups' sculptures. Have groups each briefly describe why they formed their sculpture the way they did.

Say: **The women who went to the tomb were surprised because the huge rock had been rolled away from the tomb. The symbol of the rock that's been rolled away from the tomb represents God's power to overcome great obstacles.**

Give groups each a large rock (at least three inches in diameter). Tell kids the rock symbolizes the tombstone that was rolled away from Jesus' tomb.

Say: **Have the person whose birthday is nearest to to-**

**B I B L E
A P P L I C A T I O N**
(10 to 15 minutes)

day pick up the rock and describe a "rock" or problem in his or her life that seems impossible to move. Then have the rest of your group members do the same.

Have groups then discuss the following questions:
- **How does God remove the rocks in your life?**
- **How can we help others with problems or trials?**
- **How can this rock be a symbol of hope and joy?**

Have groups each use paints and paintbrushes to turn their "tombstone" (rock) into a symbol of joy.

Have groups each display their "joy" rock for the whole group when they're done. Then form a circle and have the groups place their rocks in the center.

Ask:
- **What does Jesus' Resurrection mean to you?** (I'm free from sin; I'm going to rise again too; God loves me.)
- **How can we live with Resurrection joy every day?** (By sharing God's love with others; by thanking God each day; by loving others.)

Display the rocks in the room for a few weeks to remind kids of the joy of Jesus' Resurrection.

COMMITMENT
(10 to 15 minutes)

JOY YEAR ROUND

Say: **The joy of Jesus' Resurrection doesn't have to begin and end each Easter Sunday. Let's brainstorm practical ways to live joyfully each day.**

Give kids each a "Joy Surprise" handout (p. 44) and a pencil. Have kids complete the handouts. Then form groups of no more than four. Have kids each share their ideas with their group. Then have groups each choose three ideas to act out for the rest of the groups.

After groups each act out their ideas, say: **We can celebrate Resurrection joy in many ways, as we've just seen. Let's commit to use these ideas.**

Tape the handouts to the wall, and have kids walk around and read them. Ask kids to choose at least three ideas and commit to God to use these ideas in the coming week.

Have kids each pick up a balloon. Then form a circle. Pass a permanent marker around and have kids each write their name on their balloon. Say: **We can also celebrate Jesus' Resurrection by supporting each other.**

Walk into the center of the circle. Describe a positive trait someone in the circle has shown during the past four weeks, then present your balloon to him or her. Have that person then stand in the center of the circle and describe another person's positive trait, then give that person his or her balloon. Traits might include patience, concern for others, kindness and wisdom. Continue until each person has been in the center of the circle.

Say: **Take your balloon home with you and put it in your room. During the coming week when you look at the** balloon, say a prayer for the person whose name is written on it. Pray for that person to experience the joy of Jesus' Resurrection every day.

☐ OPTION 1: RESURRECTION JOY

Give kids each an "It's a Celebration!" handout (p. 45), a whistle and one sheet each of blue, red and green construction paper.

Say: **We're going to wrap up our course on Jesus' death and Resurrection with this celebration responsive reading. I'll read the leader's part and you'll read the people's part. When we come to an action, such as blowing the whistle, complete the action.**

After we're finished, hug at least three other people and tell them something you appreciate about them.

After the responsive reading, then join in on the hugging.

☐ OPTION 2: RESURRECTION REFLECTION

Use a sheet and string to create a hidden area in the room. You might hang the sheet diagonally in a corner of the room to create your "quiet place." Or you might simply hang the sheet over the edge of a table that's against a wall.

Say: **Jesus' death and Resurrection are powerful events in history and in our personal lives. I'd like each of us to spend a moment alone with God in this "quiet place," reflecting on the importance of Jesus' death and Resurrection. Sit quietly until I come and tap you on the shoulder. When I tap your shoulder, go to the "quiet place" and spend no more than 30 seconds in quiet prayer with God. When your prayer time is up, simply go back to your seat.**

Go around the room and silently pick kids to enter the quiet place. When everyone's been through it (including you), have kids form a circle and place their arms around each other for a group hug. Close in prayer, thanking God for sending Jesus to die for our sins and for raising him from the dead.

CLOSING
(5 to 10 minutes)

If You Still Have Time . . .

He Is Risen—Form groups of no more than five. Have groups each create a song or poem based on Matthew 28:5-7. Then have groups each perform their song or read their poem for the rest of the groups.

Course Reflection—Form a circle. Ask students to reflect on the past four lessons. Have them take turns completing the following sentences:

- Something I learned in this course was . . .
- If I could tell my friends about this course, I'd say . . .
- Something I'll do differently because of this course is . . .

JOY SURPRISE

What can you do to live out the joy of Jesus' Resurrection? In each of the boxes below, write at least two specific things you can do to live in celebration of Jesus' death and Resurrection. Use the example in the "school" box to get you started.

At school I can live with Resurrection joy by . . .
sharing my love for Jesus with one person in my English class.

At work I can live with Resurrection joy by . . .

At home I can live with Resurrection joy by . . .

With non-Christian friends I can live with Resurrection joy by . . .

With my family I can live with Resurrection joy by . . .

IT'S A CELEBRATION!

Read your part and perform the actions indicated in the parentheses.

Leader: He is risen!

People: He is risen indeed!

Leader: Let everything that has breath praise the Lord.

People: (Blow your whistles.)

Leader: We have been freed to praise and serve God.

People: We have been freed!

Leader: God's love breaks all barriers.

People: God's love breaks all barriers.

Leader: Resurrection joy brings color to the drab lives of sin we once lived in.

People: Resurrection joy is in living color!

Leader: Then praise him with the color blue . . .

People: (Hold up your blue paper and wave it in the air.)

Leader: Praise him with the color red . . .

People: (Hold up your red paper and wave it in the air.)

Leader: And praise him with the color green . . .

People: (Hold up your green paper and wave it in the air.)

Leader: Praise him together like a rainbow of promise.

People: (Hold up all the papers and wave them in the air.)

People: We are the people of promise.

Leader: God has a surprise for us. He has changed our mourning into joy.

People. We will praise God with every breath in all situations.

Leader: Praise the Lord.

All: Celebrate God's love always! Amen.

BONUS IDEAS

Passover Understanding—Invite a rabbi or another Jewish person to a meeting to discuss the significance of the Passover meal. Have kids prepare questions ahead of time to ask the guest. Kids might also want to ask the guest why Jews don't believe Jesus was the Messiah. If your kids want to ask questions such as these, tell your guest ahead of time.

Passion Week Tour—Take kids to various events at a variety of churches during Easter season. Go to a different church for each of the following events: Maundy Thursday service; Good Friday service; choir concert (or dramatic presentation); Easter sunrise service; regular Easter morning service. Meet with kids at the end of the week to discuss their experiences.

Passion Week Picture Progression—Have kids create a four-panel mural on a church wall. On each panel, have kids illustrate one of the four lessons in this course: the Last Supper; Jesus in Gethsemane; Jesus on the cross; Jesus' Resurrection. You might want kids to complete one panel a week during the four weeks leading up to Easter (presenting the final panel on Easter Sunday).

A Passion Play—Have kids create a video of Jesus' life from the time of the Passover meal with his disciples until his appearance to Mary Magdalene following his Resurrection. Have kids choose whether to portray the events as they happened in Jesus' time or modernize them. Work with kids on the script so you all feel good about presenting the finished video to the congregation.

An Act of Service—Have kids sacrifice a full Saturday to help shut-ins or other needy people in your church. Advertise the activity as a small way to thank God for his great sacrifice—sending Jesus to die for the whole world. After the activity, discuss how easy or difficult it was to sacrifice a day of fun to help others.

Easter Week Devotions—Have kids create a booklet of devotions for the days in Lent (40 days before Easter) or for Easter week. Give kids each a "Devotions" handout (p. 48) to use in creating their booklet. Encourage kids to be creative in their devotions—including scriptures to read, devotion readings (poems or kids' thoughts on the subject) and prayers in the appropriate places on the handout. Also, have kids illustrate the devotion pages. Have individuals or groups each prepare one page of the booklet. Then make copies of the completed booklet. Have kids distribute the booklets to congregation members to be used for family devotion time.

A Passion—Rent and show the video *A Passion* (Mass Media Ministries, 2116 N. Charles St., Baltimore, MD 21218). Have kids discuss the unique video and talk about how it makes them feel. Use the video to begin a study of the four gospels' approach to Jesus' death and Resurrection.

A Show of Forgiveness—Have kids prepare a slide show and dramatic reading showing God's forgiveness of our sins. Have kids present the show to the whole congregation. Include a discussion time after the event.

Table Talk—Use the "Table Talk" handout (p. 19) as the basis for a meeting with parents and teenagers. During the meeting, have parents and kids complete the handout and discuss it. Help kids lead an activity or two from each lesson in this course to help parents discuss Jesus' death and Resurrection. Have a senior pastor wrap up the meeting with a brief worship time focusing on the relevance of Jesus' death and Resurrection in our everyday lives.

Surprise Party—Plan a surprise party for kids. Don't tell kids about the party, but advertise it as a regular meeting instead. When kids arrive at the "regular meeting," surprise them with a game- and food-filled party. Discuss how they felt being surprised. Take a few minutes to compare their surprise with the wonderful surprise of Jesus' Resurrection and its importance for us today.

PARTY PLEASER

Gethsemane Retreat—Hold an overnight retreat (or lock-in) based on the theme of Matthew 26:36-46. During the retreat, have kids spend time in prayer as if they were with Jesus the night he prayed in Gethsemane. Focus the retreat on the power and importance of prayer. Have kids brainstorm concerns they have and spend small pockets of time praying for each concern.

During the retreat, have kids each find or create a "hiding place" out of cardboard boxes, tables, chairs or other items. Have kids each spend time in prayer in their hiding place during specified times throughout the retreat. Have kids prepare a worship time to end the event.

RETREAT IDEA

DEVOTIONS

Devotion for: _____

(date)

Devotion Theme: _____

Scripture to Read:

Devotion Readings:

Prayer:

Group®

Jesus' Death & Resurrection
Copyright © 1991 by Group Publishing, Inc.

Fourth Printing, 1994

Credits
Edited by Stephen Parolini
Cover designed by Jill Bendykowski and DeWain Stoll
Interior designed by Judy Atwood Bienick and Jan Aufdemberge
Illustrations by Raymond Medici
Cover photo by Brenda Rundback

ISBN 1-55945-211-0
Printed in the United States of America.